OPEN COURT READING

D1622779

SRA

A Division of The McGraw·Hill Companies

Columbus, Ohio

www.sra4kids.com

SRA/McGraw-Hill

*A Division of The **McGraw·Hill** Companies*

Copyright ©2002 by SRA/McGraw-Hill

Send all inquiries to:
SRA/McGraw-Hill
8787 Orion Place
Columbus, OH 43240-4027

Printed in the United States of America

ISBN 0-07-569553-7

2 3 4 5 6 7 8 9 QPD 06 05 04 03 02

Table of Contents

Unit 4   Fossils
Poetry and Descriptive Writing

Unit 5   Courage
Narrative Writing

Unit 6   Our Country and Its People
Persuasive Writing

Cumulative Checklists

Objective: Students get ideas for an autobiography.

Writing Your Autobiography

An autobiography tells about your life.

Prewriting

Who is the *audience* for your autobiography?

☐ your classmates

☐ your teacher

☐ your family

☐ your friend

☐ other **Should be a specific audience.** _____

What is the *purpose* of your autobiography?

☐ to tell about your life so far

☐ to tell about a special time in your life

☐ to tell about certain events in your life

☐ other **Purpose to be clear and specific.** _____

▶ **Writing Your Autobiography**

Objective: Students use a time line to help write their autobiographies.

Using a Time Line

Plan your autobiography by writing your ideas on the time line below. Remember to put your ideas in the order in which they happened.

When It Happened

Born   year   year   year

What Happened

Students should write specific information about when events occurred and specific details about what happened.

Drafting

Write the first draft of your autobiography on lined notebook paper. Use your time line to write your ideas in order. Put it in your Writing Folder.

THE WRITING PROCESS

Objective: Students revise an autobiography.

▶ **Writing Your Autobiography**

Revising

Read your autobiography. Use the checklist below to make your writing better. Use editing marks to make changes in your writing.

Ideas

☐ Will your reader understand your purpose?

☐ Are there ideas or details that need to be added?

☐ Did you leave out any important events from your life?

Organization

☐ Do your sentences tell things in order?

Word Choice

☐ Did you use clear, specific words that tell where, when, and how things happened?

Sentence Fluency

☐ Do your sentences flow clearly from one event in your life to another?

Voice

☐ Does your writing sound like *you?*

Other

☐ **Students can add other questions.**

Proofreading Marks

¶	Indent.
∧	Add something.
ℯ	Take out something.
≡	Make a capital letter.
/	Make a small letter.
sp	Check spelling.
⊙	Add a period.

Objective: Students edit and publish an autobiography.

▶ **Writing Your Autobiography**

Editing

Proofread your autobiography. Use this checklist to make sure you correct all of your mistakes.

Conventions

☐ Is every paragraph indented?

☐ Does every sentence begin with a capital letter?

☐ Did you capitalize names of people and places?

☐ Is every word spelled correctly?

☐ Does every sentence end with the correct punctuation?

☐ Other **Students can add other things to check.**

Publishing

Use this checklist to get your autobiography ready to share.

Presentation

☐ Write or type a neat copy of your autobiography.

☐ Make a cover for your autobiography. Give it a title and add a drawing or a photograph of yourself.

Other

☐ **Students can discuss and add other presentation ideas.**

THE WRITING PROCESS

UNIT 2 Kindness • **Lesson I** *Mushroom in the Rain*

Writing a Thank-You Note

Prewriting

Who is the *audience* for your note?

☐ your teacher

☐ your parent

☐ a friend

☐ other __Audience should be specific.__

What is the *purpose* of your writing?

☐ to thank someone who gave you a present

☐ to thank someone who did something kind for you

☐ other __Purpose should be clearly stated.__

Fill in the information about the person you chose.

Name: __Students may need assistance finding__
__contact names and addresses.__

Address: _____

City: _____ **State:** _____ **Zip Code:** _____

UNIT 2 Kindness • **Lesson I** *Mushroom in the Rain*

Writing

▶ **Writing a Thank-You Note**

Plan the body of your note. Write what you will include in each sentence.

1. Begin your note with a greeting.	Most thank-you notes begin with "Dear."
2. Start your letter by saying "Thank you."	Have the students begin by saying, "Thank you for . . ."
3. Tell what the person did for you.	Have the students write what the gift or help was: ". . . helping me with my art project."
4. Tell why it was important to you.	Have the students be specific about their gratitude. "Your help was important to me because . . ."
5. Choose a good closing. It could be "Thank you," "Love," or "Sincerely."	Have students choose a closing: "Love, Marcus."

Drafting

Write the first draft of your note on lined notebook paper. Put it in your Writing Folder.

P E R S O N A L   W R I T I N G

Objective: Students revise a thank-you note.

▶ **Writing a Thank-You Note**

Revising

Read your note. Use this checklist to make your note better. Use proofreading marks to make changes.

Ideas

☐ Is your reason for writing your note clear?

Organization

☐ Are your sentences in order?

Word Choice

☐ Are there other words you can use to give more detail about how you feel?

Sentence Fluency

☐ Are there sentences that do not belong because they do not stay on topic?

Voice

☐ Think about your reader. Does your note sound thankful?

Other

☐ **Can include other ideas.** _____

Make all of your changes. Add anything else your note needs.

Proofreading Marks	
¶	Indent.
∧	Add something.
ℓ	Take out something.
≡	Make a capital letter.
/	Make a small letter.
sp	Check spelling.
⊙	Add a period.

Objective: Students edit and publish a thank-you note.

UNIT 2 Kindness • **Lesson 1** *Mushroom in the Rain*

▶ **Writing a Thank-You Note**

Editing/Proofreading

Always proofread your notes. Use this checklist to make sure you remember everything.

Conventions

☐ Make sure the name and address are correct.

☐ Make sure each sentence begins with a capital letter.

☐ Check punctuation after the greeting and closing.

Publishing

Use this checklist to get your note ready to mail.

Presentation

☐ Make a card or copy your note onto a clean sheet of paper. Use your neatest handwriting.

☐ Sign your note.

☐ Read your note one more time. Make sure all the parts of the note are there.

☐ Address the envelope.

☐ Get ready to mail it or give it to your reader.

☐ Other **Students can offer other ideas.** _____

PERSONAL WRITING

Objective: Students use the writing process to write a friendly letter.

Writing a Friendly Letter

Prewriting

Who is the *audience* for your letter?

☐ a friend

☐ a relative

☐ other __Audience should be specific.__

What is the *purpose* of your writing?

☐ to tell about someone who has been kind to you

☐ to tell about a time you were kind to someone else

☐ other __Purpose should be clearly stated.__

Fill in the information about the person you chose.

Name: __Students may need assistance finding contact names and addresses.__

Address: _____

City: _____ State: _____ Zip Code: _____

UNIT 2 Kindness • **Lesson 2** *The Elves and the Shoemaker*

► **Writing a Friendly Letter**

Objective: Students use the writing process to write a friendly letter.

Writing Your Ideas

Plan the body of your letter. Write down what you will include in each sentence.

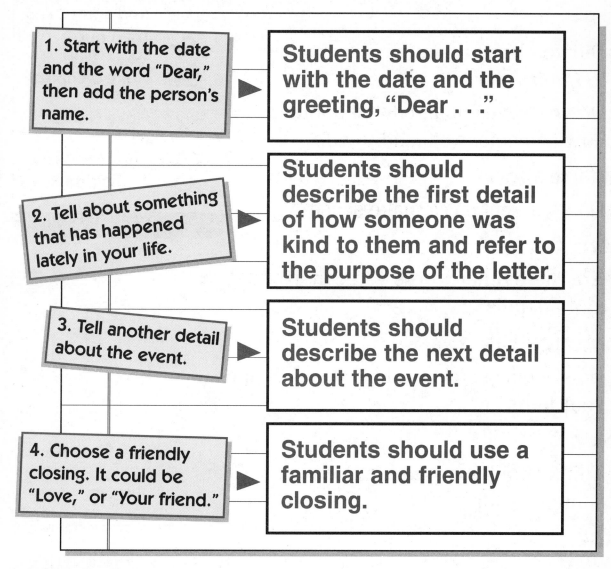

1. Start with the date and the word "Dear," then add the person's name.

► Students should start with the date and the greeting, "Dear . . ."

2. Tell about something that has happened lately in your life.

► Students should describe the first detail of how someone was kind to them and refer to the purpose of the letter.

3. Tell another detail about the event.

► Students should describe the next detail about the event.

4. Choose a friendly closing. It could be "Love," or "Your friend."

► Students should use a familiar and friendly closing.

Drafting

Write the first draft of your letter on lined notebook paper. Put it in your Writing Folder.

► **Writing a Friendly Letter**

Objective: Students revise a friendly letter.

Revising

Read your letter. Use this checklist to make your letter better. Use proofreading marks to make changes.

Proofreading Marks	
¶	Indent.
∧	Add something.
⌐e	Take out something.
=	Make a capital letter.
/	Make a small letter.
⌢sp	Check spelling.
⊙	Add a period.

Ideas

☐ Did you leave out anything you want to put in your letter?

☐ Do you have enough detail about how someone was kind to you?

Organization

☐ Do your sentences make sense?

Word Choice

☐ Are there other words you can use to give more details?

Sentence Fluency

☐ Does each sentence add a new thought to your letter?

Voice

☐ Think about your reader. Does your letter sound friendly?

Other

☐ **Students may include other ideas.**

Make all of your changes. Add anything else your letter needs.

Objective: Students edit and proofread a friendly letter.

▶ **Writing a Friendly Letter**

Editing/Proofreading

Always proofread your letters. Use this checklist to make sure you remember everything.

Conventions

☐ Make sure the name and address are correct.

☐ Make sure each sentence begins with a capital letter.

☐ Check punctuation after the greeting and closing.

Publishing

Use this checklist to get your letter ready to mail.

Presentation

☐ Copy your letter onto a clean sheet of paper. Use your neatest handwriting.

☐ Sign your letter.

☐ Read your letter one more time. Make sure all the parts of the letter are there.

☐ Address the envelope.

☐ Proofread the envelope.

☐ Get ready to mail it or give it to your reader.

☐ Other **Students can suggest other ways to publish.**

PERSONAL WRITING

UNIT 2 Kindness • **Lesson 3** *The Paper Crane*

Writing a Friendly Letter

Prewriting

Who is the *audience* for your letter?

☐ a friend

☐ a relative

☐ other __Audience should be specific.__

What is the *purpose* of your writing?

☐ to tell about an unexpected gift you received

☐ to tell about a gift you gave someone else

☐ other __Purpose should be clearly stated.__

Fill in the information about the person you chose.

Name: __Students may need assistance finding contact names and addresses.__

Address: _____

City: _____ State: _____ Zip Code: _____

▶ **Writing a Friendly Letter**

PERSONAL WRITING

Objective: Students plan and draft a friendly letter.

Writing Your Ideas

Plan the body of your letter. Write down what you will include in each sentence.

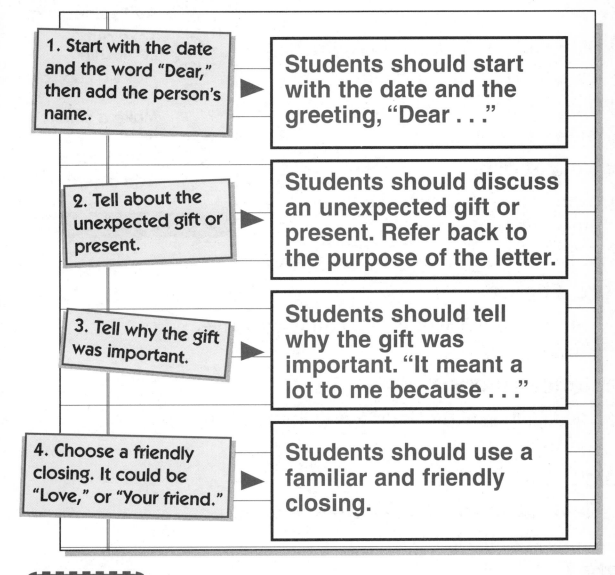

1. Start with the date and the word "Dear," then add the person's name.

▶ **Students should start with the date and the greeting, "Dear . . ."**

2. Tell about the unexpected gift or present.

▶ **Students should discuss an unexpected gift or present. Refer back to the purpose of the letter.**

3. Tell why the gift was important.

▶ **Students should tell why the gift was important. "It meant a lot to me because . . ."**

4. Choose a friendly closing. It could be "Love," or "Your friend."

▶ **Students should use a familiar and friendly closing.**

Drafting

Write the first draft of your letter on lined notebook paper. Put it in your Writing Folder.

UNIT 2 Kindness • **Lesson 3** *The Paper Crane*

► **Writing a Friendly Letter**

Objective: Students revise a friendly letter.

Revising

Read your letter. Use this checklist to make your letter better. Use proofreading marks to make changes.

Ideas

☐ Did you leave out anything you wanted to put in your letter?

☐ Did you give enough detail about the unexpected gift?

Organization

☐ Would your sentences make more sense in another order?

☐ Are all parts of your letter in place?

Word Choice

☐ Are there other words you can use to give more details?

Sentence Fluency

☐ Does each sentence add a new thought to your letter?

Voice

☐ Think about your reader. Does your letter sound friendly?

Other

☐ **Students may include other ideas.**

Make all of your changes. Add anything else your letter needs.

Proofreading Marks

¶	Indent.
∧	Add something.
ℓ	Take out something.
≡	Make a capital letter.
/	Make a small letter.
sp	Check spelling.
⊙	Add a period.

UNIT 2 Kindness • **Lesson 3** *The Paper Crane*

▶ **Writing a Friendly Letter**

Editing/Proofreading

Always proofread your letters. Use this checklist to make sure you remember everything.

Conventions

☐ Make sure the name and address are correct.

☐ Make sure each sentence begins with a capital letter.

☐ Check punctuation after the greeting and closing.

☐ Other **Students may add questions about grammar, usage, and mechanics specific to a friendly letter.**

Publishing

Use this checklist to get your letter ready to mail.

Presentation

☐ Copy your letter onto a clean sheet of paper. Use your neatest handwriting.

☐ Sign your letter.

☐ Read your letter one more time. Make sure all the parts of the letter are there.

☐ Address the envelope.

☐ Proofread the envelope.

☐ Get ready to mail it or give it to your reader.

☐ Other **Students can offer other ideas.**

PERSONAL WRITING

UNIT 2 Kindness • **Lesson 4** *Butterfly House*

Writing a Learning Log

Objective: Students get ideas for a learning log.

Prewriting

Who is the *audience* for your learning log?

☐ you

☐ a teacher

☐ other **Audience should be specific.** _____

What is the *purpose* of your writing?

☐ to write down what you observe

☐ other **Purpose should be clearly stated.** _____

Draw a picture of what you observe.

Objective: Students plan and draft a learning log.

▶ **Writing a Learning Log**

PERSONAL WRITING

Writing

Write what you observed today.

Write the date.

Write what you observe.

Include details about what you learn or observe.

▼   ▼   ▼

Date	Subject	Description

Write the first entry of your learning log.

Objective: Students continue writing in learning log.

▶ **Writing a Learning Log**

Writing

Continue writing your learning log.

Write the date.

Write what you observe.

Include details about what you learn or observe.

▼   ▼   ▼

Date	Subject	Description

PERSONAL WRITING

▶ **Writing a Learning Log**

Objective: Students edit, proofread, and publish a learning log.

Editing/Proofreading

Proofread your learning log. Use this checklist to make sure you remember everything.

Conventions

☐ Make sure you have the date of each entry.

☐ Make sure you name the topic.

☐ Make sure you have clear notes about your topic.

☐ Make sure you add any questions you have about your topic.

Publishing

Use this checklist to finish your learning log.

Presentation

☐ Copy your learning log onto a clean sheet of paper. Use your neatest handwriting.

☐ Draw pictures to make your learning log more understandable to your readers.

☐ Share your learning log with your classmates.

☐ Put your learning log in a class collection.

☐ Other **Students can offer other ideas.** _____

UNIT 2 Kindness • **Lesson 5** *Corduroy/April Medicine*

Writing a Journal

Objective: Students get ideas for a journal.

Students learn about a journal and create one of their own.

Prewriting

Who is the *audience* for your journal?

☐ you

☐ a teacher

☐ other **Audience should be specific.**

What is the *purpose* of your writing?

☐ to write about things that happen to you

☐ to write about what matters to you

☐ to make a list

☐ other **Purpose should be clearly stated.**

Objective: Students write in a journal.

▶ Writing a Journal

Plan your entries. Write down what you will include in your journal.

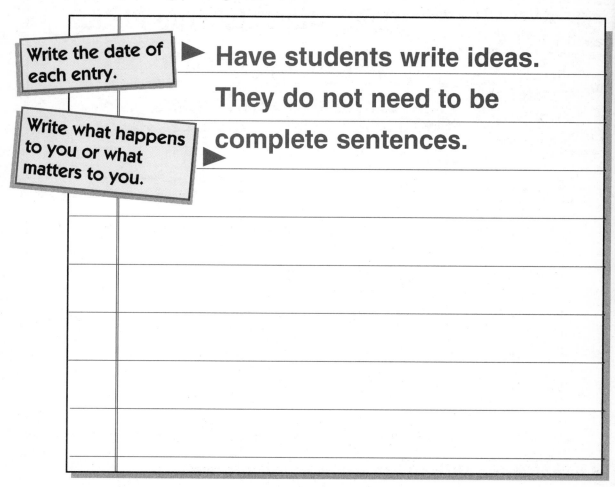

Write the date of each entry.

Write what happens to you or what matters to you.

▶ Have students write ideas.
They do not need to be
complete sentences.

PERSONAL WRITING

Write the first entry of your journal on lined notebook paper.

Here are some ideas for your entries

☐ Write about something that made you happy yesterday.

☐ Write about something that is important to you.

UNIT 2 Kindness • **Lesson 5** *Corduroy/April Medicine*

▶ **Writing a Journal**

Objective: Students continue to write in a journal.

Continue writing in your journal.

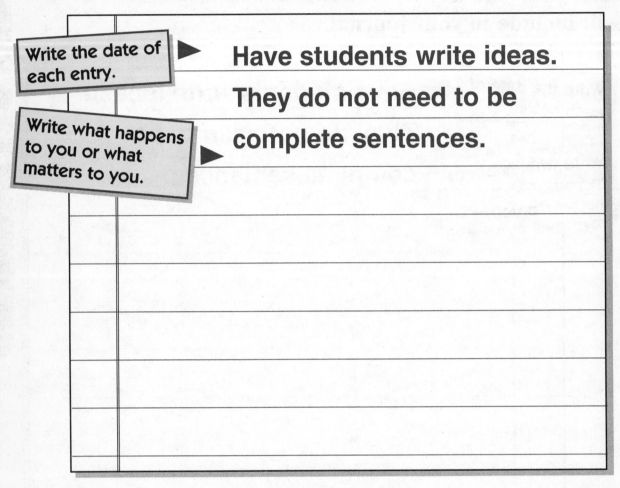

Write the date of each entry.

▶ Have students write ideas.

They do not need to be

Write what happens to you or what matters to you.

▶ complete sentences.

Here are some kinds of lists you could write.

☐ Make a list of all the people you talked to yesterday.

☐ Make a list of things you want to do this weekend.

☐ Make a list of your favorite books, television shows, or movies.

UNIT 2 Kindness • **Lesson 5** *Corduroy/April Medicine*

Objective: Students continue to write in a journal.

PERSONAL WRITING

▶ **Writing a Journal**

Continue writing in your journal.

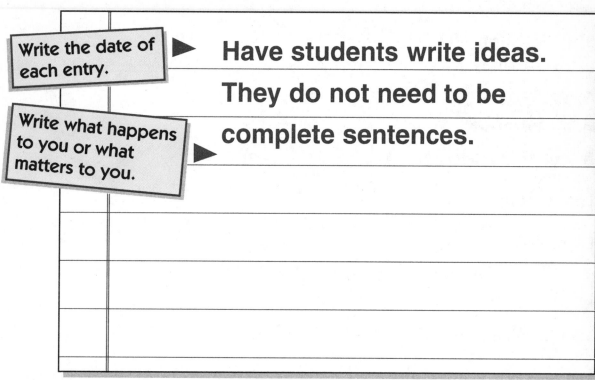

Write the date of each entry. ▶ Have students write ideas. They do not need to be complete sentences.

Write what happens to you or what matters to you. ▶

What are some good reasons for keeping a journal?

remember things, write how I feel

_____

_____

How could a journal help you?

remember things, keep memories

_____

_____

UNIT 2 Kindness • **Lesson 6** *The Story of Three Whales*

Writing a Business Letter

Students use the writing process to write a business letter.

Prewriting

Who is the *audience* for your letter?

☐ a company

☐ a person

☐ other **Audience should be specific.**

What is the *purpose* of your writing?

☐ to ask for something

☐ to share your ideas about something

☐ other **Purpose should be clearly stated.**

Fill in information about the person you chose.

Name: **Students may need assistance finding contact names and addresses.**

Address: _____

City: _____ **State:** _____ **Zip Code:** _____

UNIT 2 Kindness • **Lesson 6** *The Story of Three Whales*

Objective: Students plan and draft a business letter.

Writing

▶ **Writing a Business Letter**

1. Heading: Start with your name and address. ▶

2. Inside Address: Add the name and address of the person to whom you are writing. ▶

3. Greeting: Start with the words "To Whom it May Concern" or "Dear," then add the person's name. ▶

4. Body: Ask for something or share your ideas. ▶

5. Closing: End your letter with "Yours truly" or "Sincerely." ▶

6. Signature: Write your first and last name. ▶

Have students write ideas.

They do not need to be

complete sentences.

Drafting

Write the first draft on lined notebook paper.

PERSONAL WRITING

Writing a Business Letter

Objective: Students revise a business letter.

Revising

Read your letter. Use this checklist to make your letter better. Use proofreading marks to make changes.

Ideas

☐ Is your reason for writing the letter clear?

☐ Do you have enough detail about what you want to say?

Organization

☐ Did you stay on the topic?

☐ Are all parts of your letter in place?

Word Choice

☐ Are there other words you can use to give more detail about what you want to say?

Sentence Fluency

☐ Are there sentences you can delete?

Voice

☐ Is your letter polite?

Other

☐ **Students may include other ideas.**

Proofreading Marks	
¶	Indent.
∧	Add something.
ℓ	Take out something.
≡	Make a capital letter.
/	Make a small letter.
sp	Check spelling.
⊙	Add a period.

UNIT 2 Kindness • **Lesson 6** *The Story of Three Whales*

PERSONAL WRITING

Editing/Proofreading

▶ **Writing a Business Letter**

Always proofread your letters. Use this checklist to make sure you remember everything.

Conventions

☐ Make sure the name and address are correct.

☐ Make sure each sentence begins with a capital letter.

☐ Check punctuation after the greeting and closing.

☐ Other __Students may add other questions.__

Publishing

Use this checklist to get your letter ready to mail.

Presentation

☐ Copy your letter onto a clean sheet of paper. Use your neatest handwriting.

☐ Sign your letter.

☐ Read your letter one more time. Make sure all the parts of the letter are there.

☐ Address the envelope.

☐ Proofread the envelope.

☐ Get ready to mail your letter.

Name _____ Date _____

Writing Lists, Invitations, and Notes

Objective: Students plan writing lists, invitations, and notes.

Who is the *audience*?

☐ you

☐ a friend

☐ a family member

☐ other **Audience should be specific.** _____

What is the *purpose* of your writing?

☐ to invite someone to a party or event

☐ to tell someone something or thank someone

☐ other **Purpose should be clearly stated.** _____

Objective: Students write a list.

PERSONAL WRITING

Planning

▶ **Writing Lists**

Plan your list. Write down what you will include in your list.

Write the names of the people or things you want on your list.	Have students write ideas. They do not need to be in complete sentences.
1.	
2.	
3.	
4.	
5.	
6.	
7.	
8.	
9.	
10.	

Write the first draft of your list on a sheet of paper and put it in your Writing Folder.

Name _____ Date _____

Planning

Plan your invitation. Write down the important information below.

> Be sure to tell the reason for the party. Also tell the time, date, and place of the party.

Party

For: _____

_____

Time: _____

Date: _____

Place: _____

_____

_____

_____

Write your invitation and put it in your Writing Folder.

Objective: Students write an invitation.

UNIT 2 Kindness • **Lesson 7** *Cinderella*

Planning

Plan an RSVP note. Think about what you are going to say.

RSVP

Be sure to tell if you plan to go to the event.

Write your RSVP and put it in your Writing Folder.

Objective: Students write a note.

PERSONAL WRITING

Objective: Students get ideas for their paragraph.

Writing Paragraphs That Explain

Prewriting

Who is the *audience* for your paragraph?

☐ your classmates

☐ your teacher

☐ your family

☐ a friend

☐ other __Audience should be specific.__

What is the *purpose* of your paragraph?

☐ to explain something

☐ other __Purpose should be specific.__

Name _____ Date _____

Objective: Students choose a topic and begin to write a paragraph.

EXPOSITORY WRITING

▶ Writing Paragraphs That Explain

You need to choose a topic that you know about. Fill in the web with information.

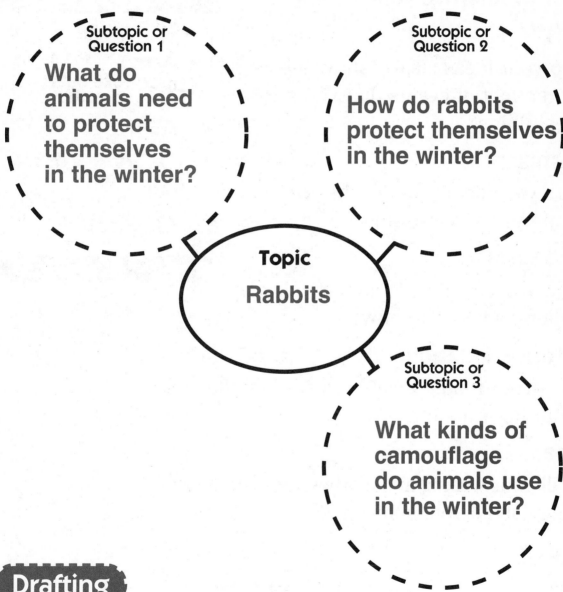

Subtopic or Question 1

What do animals need to protect themselves in the winter?

Subtopic or Question 2

How do rabbits protect themselves in the winter?

Topic

Rabbits

Subtopic or Question 3

What kinds of camouflage do animals use in the winter?

Drafting

Write the first draft of your writing on lined notebook paper. Use your web to make sure all your ideas are organized in a clear way. Put it in your Writing Folder.

Objective: Students revise their paragraphs.

Writing Paragraphs That Explain

Revising

Read your writing. Use the checklist below to improve your writing.

Ideas

☐ Do your ideas clearly show the cause and effect of events that you are describing?

Organization

☐ Are your details under the correct subtopic or question?

Word Choice

☐ Did you use good facts that tell what, where, when, and how?

Sentence Fluency

☐ Will your reader be able to easily understand your information?

Voice

☐ Will your writing make others want to learn more about your subject?

Other

☐ **Students should add any other questions.**

Proofreading Marks

¶	Indent.
∧	Add something.
ℒ	Take out something.
≡	Make a capital letter.
/	Make a small letter.
⟲sp	Check spelling.
⊙	Add a period.

Objective: Students edit and proofread their paragraphs.

▶ **Writing Paragraphs That Explain**

Editing/Proofreading

Proofread your paragraph. Use this checklist to help you correct any mistakes.

Conventions

☐ Is the paragraph indented?

☐ Does every sentence begin with a capital letter?

☐ Are all proper nouns capitalized?

☐ Are all words and special terms spelled correctly?

☐ Does every sentence end with the correct punctuation?

☐ Other **Students should include any other questions.**

Publishing

Use this checklist to get your paragraph ready to share.

Presentation

☐ Write or type a neat copy of your paragraph.

☐ Include drawings, diagrams, or photographs to help tell about your topic.

☐ Other **Add other ideas for presentation.**

EXPOSITORY WRITING

UNIT 3 Look Again • **Lesson 2** *They Thought They Saw Him*

Objective: Students get ideas for writing a paragraph.

Explaining How Something Happens

Prewriting

Who is the *audience* for your paragraph?

☐ your classmates

☐ your teacher

☐ your family

☐ a friend

☐ other **Audience should be specific.**

What is the *purpose* of your paragraph?

☐ to explain how something happens

☐ other **Purpose for the writing needs to be clear and specific.**

Name _____ Date _____

Expository Writing (vertical, right margin)

▶ **Explaining How Something Happens**

Objective: Students plan and draft their paragraphs. (vertical, left margin)

Plan your paragraph by writing your ideas on the map below. Remember to put your ideas in order.

> **First a chameleon is spotted by an enemy.**

> **Then it changes the color of its skin.**

> **It is protected from the enemy.**

Drafting

Write the first draft of your paragraph on lined notebook paper. Follow your prewriting map. Put it in your Writing Folder.

Objective: Students revise their paragraphs.

▶ Explaining How Something Happens

Revising

Read your explanation. Use the checklist below to make your writing better. Use proofreading marks to make changes in your writing.

Ideas

☐ Are there any ideas or details that need to be added?

Organization

☐ Do your sentences describe steps in the correct order?

Word Choice

☐ Did you correctly use time and order words?

Sentence Fluency

☐ Do your sentences flow clearly from one step to another?

Voice

☐ Does your writing sound as if you were explaining how something happens?

Other

☐ **Students should add any other concerns.**

Proofreading Marks	
¶	Indent.
∧	Add something.
℮	Take out something.
≡	Make a capital letter.
/	Make a small letter.
sp	Check spelling.
⊙	Add a period.

Objective: Students edit and proofread their paragraphs.

EXPOSITORY WRITING

▶ **Explaining How Something Happens**

Editing/Proofreading

pinky

Proofread your paragraph. Use this checklist to make sure you catch all of your mistakes.

Conventions

☐ Does every sentence begin with a capital letter?

☐ Is every word correctly spelled?

☐ Does every sentence end with the correct punctuation?

☐ Other **Students should include any other concerns.**

Publishing

Use this checklist to get your paragraph ready to share.

Presentation

☐ Write or type a neat copy of your paragraph.

☐ Include a drawing or a map that shows the steps in the right order.

☐ Other **Add ideas for presentation that you and the class have discussed.**

UNIT 3 Look Again • **Lesson 3** *Hungry Little Hare*

Objective: Students get ideas for writing their book review.

Writing a Fiction Book Review

Prewriting

Who is the *audience* for your book review?

☐ your school

☐ your classmates

☐ your teacher

☐ your family

☐ a friend

☐ other __Audience should be specific.__

What is the *purpose* of your book review?

☐ to tell about the characters and plot of a fiction book

☐ to tell your feelings about the fiction book

☐ to get others to read your book

☐ other __Purpose should be clear and specific.__

Name _____ Date _____

▶ **Writing a Fiction Book Review**

EXPOSITORY WRITING

Plan your review. Answer each question shown below.

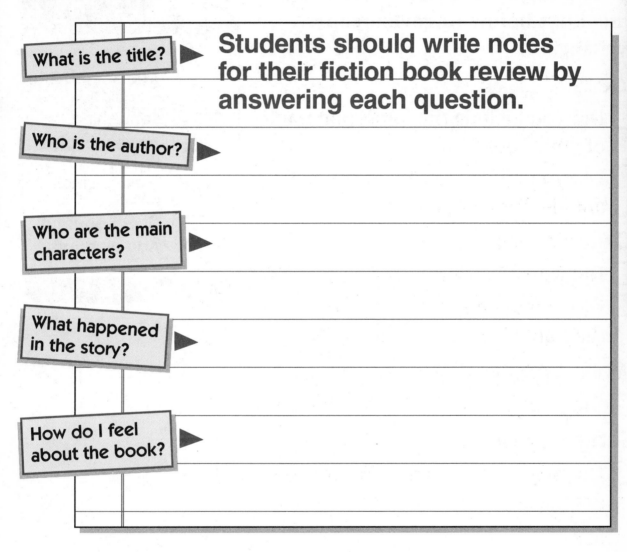

What is the title? ▶ Students should write notes for their fiction book review by answering each question.

Who is the author? ▶

Who are the main characters? ▶

What happened in the story? ▶

How do I feel about the book? ▶

Drafting

Write the first draft of your book review on lined notebook paper.

▶ **Writing a Fiction Book Review**

Objective: Students revise their book reviews.

Revising

Read your book review. Use the checklist below to revise your writing.

Ideas

☐ Did you include the important parts of your book?

☐ Did you include the correct names and details from your book?

Organization

☐ Did you tell about the events in order?

☐ Did you tell how you feel about the book?

Word Choice

☐ Did you use correct facts and names?

Sentence Fluency

☐ Do your sentences flow from one event to another?

Voice

☐ Does your writing make others want to read the book?

Other

☐ **Students should add any other questions.**

Proofreading Marks	
¶	Indent.
∧	Add something.
ℓ	Take out something.
≡	Make a capital letter.
/	Make a small letter.
sp	Check spelling.
⊙	Add a period.

▶ Writing a Fiction Book Review

Objective: Students edit and proofread their book reviews.

EXPOSITORY WRITING

Editing/Proofreading

Proofread your book review. Use this checklist to help you find any mistakes in your writing.

Conventions

☐ Did you indent the paragraph?

☐ Does every sentence begin with a capital letter?

☐ Did you capitalize characters' names, place names, and book titles?

☐ Did you underline the title of your book?

☐ Is every word spelled correctly?

☐ Does every sentence end with the correct punctuation?

☐ Other **Students should include any other questions.**

Publishing

Use this checklist to get your fiction book review ready to share.

Presentation

☐ Write or type a neat copy of your book review.

☐ Have the book or book cover to share.

☐ Other **Add ideas for presentation.**

UNIT 3   Look Again • **Lesson 4** *How to Hide an Octopus*

Writing a Report

Objective: Students get ideas for their reports.

Prewriting

Who is the *audience* for your report?

☐ your classmates

☐ your teacher

☐ your school newspaper

☐ your family

☐ a friend

☐ other **Audience should be specific.** _____

What is the *purpose* of your report?

☐ to tell others about a subject that interests you

☐ other **Purpose for the writing needs to be clear and specific.** _____

Sheepherding
in
New Zealand
by
Jamie Wells

Objective: Students make a plan and begin to write their reports.

► **Writing a Report**

EXPOSITORY WRITING

Plan your report by choosing your topic and asking three questions about your topic. Then write the facts on the web below.

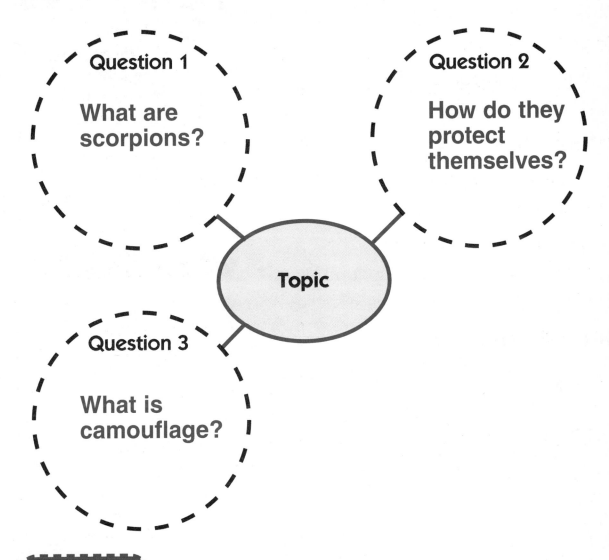

Question 1

What are scorpions?

Question 2

How do they protect themselves?

Topic

Question 3

What is camouflage?

Drafting

Write the first draft of your report on lined notebook paper. Follow your prewriting notes to make sure you answer each question about your topic.

Objective: Students revise their reports.

Revising

▶ **Writing a Report**

Read your report. Use the checklist below to make your writing better.

Ideas

☐ Did you answer all of your questions?

Organization

☐ Do you have one paragraph for each question?

Word Choice

☐ Did you use facts and special words correctly?

Sentence Fluency

☐ Do your ideas and information flow smoothly from one sentence to another?

Voice

☐ Is your report written in an interesting, lively way?

Other

☐ **Students should add any other questions.**

Proofreading Marks

¶	Indent.
∧	Add something.
ℓ	Take out something.
≡	Make a capital letter.
/	Make a small letter.
sp	Check spelling.
⊙	Add a period.

▶ **Writing a Report**

EXPOSITORY WRITING

Objective: Students edit and proofread their reports.

Editing/Proofreading

Proofread your report. Use this checklist to help you correct mistakes in your writing.

Conventions

☐ Did you indent every paragraph?

☐ Does every sentence begin with a capital letter?

☐ Did you capitalize people's names and place names?

☐ Are all words and special names and terms spelled correctly?

☐ Does every sentence end with the correct punctuation?

☐ Other ___**Students should include any other questions.**___

Publishing

Use this checklist to get your report ready to share.

Presentation

☐ Write or type a neat copy of your report.

☐ Include a drawing, photograph, or other visual aid to go with your report.

☐ Read aloud your report to the whole class or to small groups of classmates.

☐ Other ___**Add ideas for presentation.**___

Objective: Students get ideas about writing their directions.

Writing Directions

Prewriting

Who is the *audience* for your paragraph?

☐ your classmates

☐ your teacher

☐ your family

☐ a friend

☐ other <u>**Audience should be specific.**</u>

What is the *purpose* of your paragraph?

☐ to give directions that tell how to get to a
certain place

☐ other <u>**Purpose for the writing needs**</u>
to be clear and specific.

EXPOSITORY WRITING

▶ **Writing Directions**

Objective: Students plan and begin writing their directions.

Plan a paragraph that gives directions.
Remember to put your ideas in order.

First	**The guinea fowl talks to her friend the cow.**
Second	**The cow gives her spots with milk.**
Then	**She walks past the lion with her spots.**
Finally	**She is safe and goes home.**

Drafting

Write the first draft of your directions on
lined notebook paper. Follow your
prewriting map to write your directions.

Objective: Students revise their directions.

Revising

Writing Directions

Read your directions. Use the checklist below to make your writing better.

Ideas

☐ Are there any details that need to be added to make the directions clear?

Organization

☐ Do your directions begin from the location of the reader?

☐ Do your sentences describe the steps to take in the correct order?

Word Choice

☐ Did you correctly use location words?

Sentence Fluency

☐ Will your reader be able to easily follow the directions?

Voice

☐ Did you tell about each step in a clear way?

Other

☐ **Students should add any other questions.**

Proofreading Marks

⊬	Indent.
∧	Add something.
ℓ	Take out something.
≡	Make a capital letter.
/	Make a small letter.
⌇	Check spelling.
⊙	Add a period.

▶ **Writing Directions**

Editing/Proofreading

Proofread your directions. Use this checklist to help you correct all of your mistakes.

Conventions

☐ Does every sentence begin with a capital letter?

☐ Is every word spelled correctly?

☐ Other **Students should include any other questions.**

Publishing

Use this checklist to get your paragraph ready to share.

Presentation

☐ Write or type a neat copy of your paragraph.

☐ Include a drawing or a map that shows the directions in the right order.

☐ Ask someone to see if they can follow your directions.

☐ Other **Add ideas for presentation.**

Objective: Students edit and proofread their directions.

EXPOSITORY WRITING

Name _____ Date _____

Writing a Nonfiction Book Review

Prewriting

Who is the *audience* for your nonfiction book review?

☐ your school

☐ your classmates

☐ your teacher

☐ your family

☐ a friend

☐ other **Audience should be specific.**

What is the *purpose* of your nonfiction book review?

☐ to tell about the nonfiction book

☐ to tell how you feel about the book

☐ to get others to want to read your book

☐ other **Purpose should be clear and specific.**

UNIT 3 Look Again • **Lesson 6** *Animal Camouflage*

Objective: Students plan and begin to write their book reviews.

▶ Writing a Nonfiction Book Review

EXPOSITORY WRITING

Plan your nonfiction book review by answering each question.

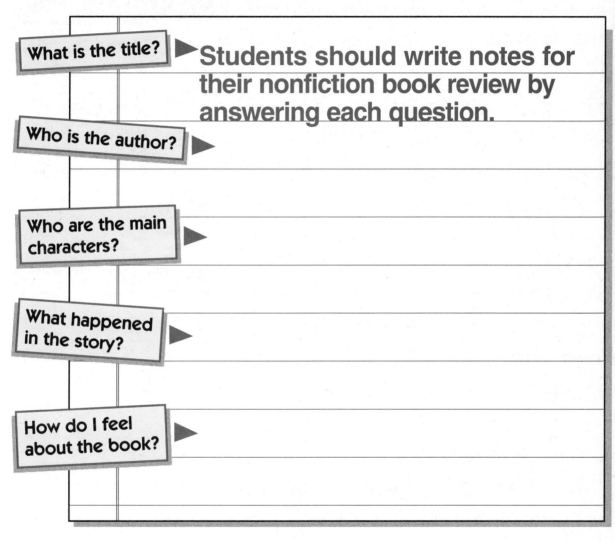

What is the title? ▶ Students should write notes for their nonfiction book review by answering each question.

Who is the author? ▶

Who are the main characters? ▶

What happened in the story? ▶

How do I feel about the book? ▶

Drafting

Write the first draft of your nonfiction book review on lined notebook paper.

Name ______________________ Date __________

Writing a Nonfiction Book Review

Revising

Objective: Students revise their book reviews.

Read your nonfiction book review. Use the checklist below to improve your writing.

Proofreading Marks

¶	Indent.
^	Add something.
℘	Take out something.
≡	Make a capital letter.
/	Make a small letter.
sp	Check spelling.
⊙	Add a period.

Ideas

☐ Did you write about the most important parts of your book?

Organization

☐ Did you introduce the book by title and author at the beginning of your review?

☐ Did you remember to tell how you feel about the book and why?

Word Choice

☐ Did you use correct facts and names of people and places from the book?

Sentence Fluency

☐ Will your reader be able to understand what you are saying?

Voice

☐ Do your words show how you feel about the book?

Other

☐ **Students should add any other questions.**

EXPOSITORY WRITING

▶ **Writing a Nonfiction Book Review**

Objective: Students edit and proofread their book reviews.

Editing/Proofreading

Proofread your nonfiction book review. Use this checklist to find any mistakes in your writing.

Conventions

☐ Did you indent every paragraph?

☐ Does every sentence begin with a capital letter?

☐ Did you capitalize people's names, place names, and book titles?

☐ Did you underline the title of your book?

☐ Is every word spelled correctly?

☐ Does every sentence end with the correct punctuation?

☐ Other ___Students should include any other questions.___

Publishing

Use this checklist to get your nonfiction book review ready to share.

Presentation

☐ Write or type a neat copy of your book review.

☐ Have the book with you to share.

☐ Other ___Add ideas for presentation.___

Objective: Students write an acrostic poem.

Writing an Acrostic Poem

Prewriting

Who is the *audience* for your poem?

☐ your teacher

☐ a family member

☐ a friend

☐ other ___ **Audience should be specific.** ___

What is the *purpose* of your poem?

☐ to tell about dinosaurs

☐ to tell about fossils

☐ other ___ **Answers will vary.** ___

What word will you use for your acrostic?

☐ FOSSIL

☐ DINOSAUR

☐ other ___ **Word should be simple.** ___

Writing an Acrostic Poem

Plan your poem. Write down ideas or phrases for each letter you are using. Have students write ideas. They do not need to be complete sentences.

Objective: Students prewrite their poems.

Write the word you want to use for your poem down this side of the line.

Write the new words you want to form from each letter on the left-hand side.

POETRY

Drafting

Write the first draft of your poem on lined notebook paper.

UNIT 4   **Fossils • Lesson I** *Fossils Tell of Long Ago*

Objective: Students revise their poems.

Revising

▶ **Writing an Acrostic Poem**

Read your poem. Use this checklist to make your poem better. Use proofreading marks to make changes.

Ideas

☐ Did you choose an easy word for your poem?

☐ Do the words you used tell about your topic?

☐ Other **Can include additional questions.**

Organization

☐ Are your ideas clear?

☐ Did you stay on topic?

☐ Are all the words or phrases for each letter on the topic?

Word Choice

☐ Did you use good describing words?

☐ Are there other words you can use to give more detail about your topic?

Proofreading Marks

¶	Indent.
∧	Add something.
ℓ	Take out something.
≡	Make a capital letter.
/	Make a small letter.
sp	Check spelling.
⊙	Add a period.

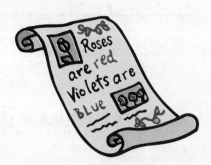

UNIT 4 Fossils • **Lesson I** *Fossils Tell of Long Ago*

Objective: Students edit and proofread a poem.

► **Writing an Acrostic Poem**

Editing/Proofreading

Always proofread your poems. Use this checklist to help you remember everything.

Conventions

☐ Make sure words are spelled correctly.

☐ Make sure the first letter on every line is capitalized.

☐ Other **Can add other questions.** _____

Publishing

Use this checklist to complete your poem.

Presentation

☐ Read your poem one more time. Make sure all the parts are there.

☐ Copy your poem onto a clean sheet of paper. Use your neatest handwriting.

☐ Can you draw pictures of the word or words in your poem?

POETRY

Writing a Pattern Poem

Objective: Students write a pattern poem.

Prewriting

Who is the *audience* for your poem?

☐ your classmates

☐ your teacher

☐ school newspaper

☐ Other **Audience should be specific.**

What is the *purpose* of your pattern poem?

☐ to tell about dinosaurs

☐ to tell about fossils

☐ Other **Topic should be clearly stated.**

What familiar song or poem are you going to use for your pattern poem?

☐ Itsy, Bitsy Spider

☐ Mary Had a Little Lamb

☐ Row, Row, Row Your Boat

☐ Other **Song should be simple and familiar.**

UNIT 4 Fossils • **Lesson 2** *The Dinosaurs Who Lived in My Backyard*

► **Writing a Pattern Poem**

Objectives: Students plan and draft a pattern poem.

P O E T R Y

Plan your poem. Write down what you will include in your poem. Have students write ideas. They do not need to be complete sentences.

Write the poem or song after which you want to pattern your poem. ►

Write the new words you came up with for your poem. Make sure your new poem fits the rhyme and rhythm of the first poem or song. ►

Drafting

Write the first draft of your poem on lined notebook paper.

Objective: Students revise a poem.

▶ **Writing a Pattern Poem**

Revising

Read your poem. Use this checklist to make your poem better. Use proofreading marks to make changes.

Ideas

☐ Did you choose a familiar song or poem?

☐ Do the words you chose tell about your topic?

☐ Other **Can include additional questions.**

Organization

☐ Are your ideas clear?

☐ Did you stay on your topic?

Word Choice

☐ Did you use words that fit the pattern of your song or poem?

☐ Are there other words you can use to give more detail about your topic?

☐ Did you use rhyme, alliteration, repetition, onomatopoeia, and/or rhythm?

Make all of your changes. Add anything else your poem needs.

Proofreading Marks	
¶	Indent.
∧	Add something.
ℓ	Take out something.
≡	Make a capital letter.
/	Make a small letter.
⊸ℓ	Check spelling.
⊙	Add a period.

UNIT 4 Fossils • **Lesson 2** *The Dinosaurs Who Lived in My Backyard*

Objective: Students edit and proofread a poem.

▶ **Writing a Pattern Poem**

Editing/Proofreading

Always proofread your poems. Use this checklist to help you remember everything.

Conventions

☐ Make sure words are spelled correctly.

☐ Make sure all proper nouns are capitalized.

☐ Other **Can add other questions.**

Publishing

Use this checklist to complete your poem.

Presentation

☐ Read your poem one more time. Make sure all the parts are there.

☐ Copy your poem onto a clean sheet of paper. Use your neatest handwriting.

☐ Draw a picture of the topic of your poem.

POETRY

UNIT 4   Fossils • **Lesson 3** *Dinosaur Fossils*

Writing a Free-Verse Poem

Prewriting

Who is the *audience* for your poem?

☐ your teacher

☐ a family member

☐ a friend

☐ other **Audience should be specific.** _____

What is the *purpose* of your poem?

☐ to tell about a visit to the museum

☐ to tell about fossils

☐ to tell about dinosaurs

☐ other **Topic should be specific.** _____

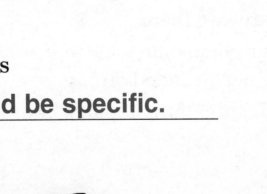

▶ **Writing a Free-Verse Poem**

Writing Your Poem

Plan your poem. Write down what you will include in your poem.

Have students write ideas.
They do not need to be
complete sentences.

Objective: Students plan and draft a poem.

P O E T R Y

Drafting

Write the first draft of your poem on lined notebook paper. Put it in your Writing Folder.

Objective: Students revise a poem.

Writing a Free-Verse Poem

Revising

Read your poem. Use this checklist to make your poem better.

Ideas

☐ Did you use interesting ideas in your poem?

☐ Do the words you chose tell about your topic?

☐ Other **Can include additional questions.**

Organization

☐ Are your ideas clear?

☐ Did you stay on your topic?

Word Choice

☐ Did you use figurative language like similes and metaphors?

☐ Are there other words you can use to give more detail about your topic?

Make all of your changes. Add anything else your poem needs.

Proofreading Marks

¶	Indent.
∧	Add something.
ℓ	Take out something.
≡	Make a capital letter.
/	Make a small letter.
sp	Check spelling.
⊙	Add a period.

UNIT 4 Fossils • **Lesson 3** *Dinosaur Fossils*

Objective: Students edit and proofread a poem.

POETRY

▶ **Writing a Free-Verse Poem**

Editing/Proofreading

Always proofread your poems. Use this checklist to make sure you remember everything.

Conventions

☐ Make sure words are spelled correctly.

☐ Make sure all the proper nouns are capitalized.

☐ Other **Can add other questions.** _____

Publishing

Use this checklist to complete your poem.

Presentation

☐ Read your poem one more time.

☐ Copy your poem onto a clean sheet of paper. Use your neatest handwriting.

☐ Draw pictures to make your poem more interesting.

☐ Print a copy of your poem on the computer at school.

Writing a Descriptive Paragraph

Prewriting

Who is the *audience* for your paragraph?

☐ your teacher

☐ a family member

☐ a friend

☐ other **Audience should be specific.**

What is the *purpose* of your paragraph?

☐ to describe how meteorites may have made the dinosaurs extinct

☐ to describe how the weather may have made the dinosaurs extinct

☐ other **Answers should include a reason dinosaurs are extinct.**

Name _____ Date _____

▶ **Writing a Descriptive Paragraph**

Objective: Students plan and draft a paragraph.

Plan the body of your paragraph. Write down what you will include in each sentence. **Have students write ideas.**

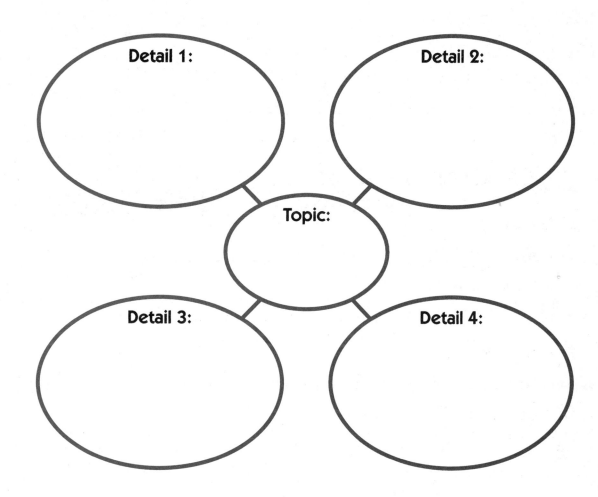

Detail 1:

Detail 2:

Topic:

Detail 3:

Detail 4:

DESCRIPTIVE WRITING

⌐**Drafting**⌐

Write the first draft of your paragraph on lined notebook paper.

▶ **Writing a Descriptive Paragraph**

Objective: Students revise a paragraph.

Revising

Read your paragraph. Use this checklist to make your paragraph better. Use proofreading marks to make changes.

Ideas

☐ Did you leave out anything you wanted to put in your paragraph?

☐ Do you give enough detail about the topic?

☐ Other **Can include other questions.**

Proofreading Marks	
¶	Indent.
∧	Add something.
ℓ	Take out something.
≡	Make a capital letter.
/	Make a small letter.
ꞩℓ	Check spelling.
⊙	Add a period.

Organization

☐ Are your sentences in the order that the events happened?

☐ Are all parts of your paragraph in place?

Word Choice

☐ Are there other words you can use to give more detail about the topic?

☐ Do the words you used give good descriptions?

Sentence Fluency

☐ Does each sentence add a new thought to your paragraph?

☐ Are there sentences you can delete?

Make all of your changes. Add anything else your paragraph needs.

▶ **Writing a Descriptive Paragraph**

Objective: Students edit and proofread a paragraph.

DESCRIPTIVE WRITING

Editing/Proofreading

Always proofread your paragraphs. Use this checklist to make sure you remember everything.

Conventions

☐ Make sure the sentences are complete.

☐ Make sure each sentence begins with a capital letter.

☐ Make sure the first sentence is indented.

☐ Other __**Can add other questions.**__

Publishing

Use this checklist to complete your paragraph.

Presentation

☐ Read your paragraph one more time. Make sure all the parts are there.

☐ Copy your paragraph onto a clean sheet of paper. Use your neatest handwriting.

☐ Draw pictures of your topic.

UNIT 4   Fossils • **Lesson 5** *Monster Tracks*

Prewriting

Objective: Students write a descriptive paragraph.

Who is the *audience* for your paragraph?

☐ your teacher

☐ a family member

☐ a friend

☐ other **Audience should be specific.**

What is the *purpose* of your paragraph?

☐ to describe how fossils are made

☐ to describe how anyone can make fossils

☐ other **Topic should describe fossils in some way.**

DESCRIPTIVE WRITING

▶ Writing a Descriptive Paragraph

Plan the body of your paragraph. Write down what you will include in each sentence.

Objective: Students plan and draft a paragraph.

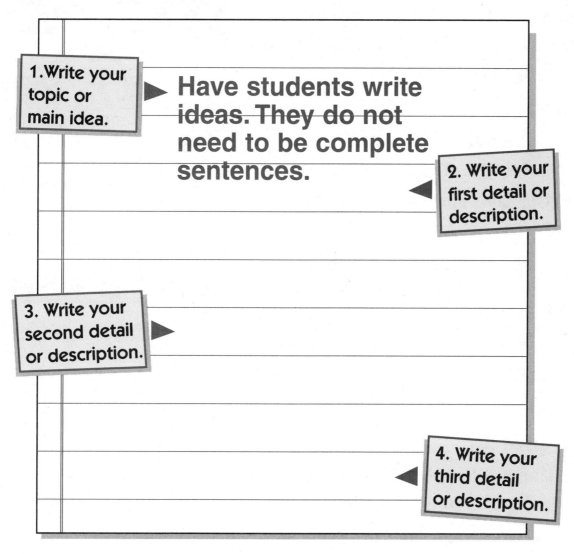

1. Write your topic or main idea.

Have students write ideas. They do not need to be complete sentences.

2. Write your first detail or description.

3. Write your second detail or description.

4. Write your third detail or description.

Drafting

Write the first draft of your paragraph on lined notebook paper.

▶ **Writing a Descriptive Paragraph**

Revising

Read your paragraph. Use this checklist to make your paragraph better. Use proofreading marks to make changes.

Ideas

☐ Did you leave out anything you wanted to put in your paragraph?

☐ Do you have enough detail about the topic?

☐ Other **Can include additional questions.**

Organization

☐ Are your sentences in the order that the events happen?

☐ Are all parts of your paragraph in place?

Word Choice

☐ Are there other words you can use to give more detail about the topic?

☐ Do the words you used give good descriptions?

Sentence Fluency

☐ Does each sentence add a new thought to your paragraph?

☐ Are there sentences you can delete?

Make all of your changes. Add anything else your paragraph needs.

Proofreading Marks

¶ Indent.
∧ Add something.
℮ Take out something.
≡ Make a capital letter.
／ Make a small letter.
sp Check spelling.
⊙ Add a period.

Objective: Students revise a paragraph.

▶ **Writing a Descriptive Paragraph**

DESCRIPTIVE WRITING

Objective: Students edit and proofread a paragraph.

Editing/Proofreading

Always proofread your paragraphs. Use this checklist to make sure you remember everything.

Conventions

☐ Check the end marks of all sentences.

☐ Make sure each sentence begins with a capital letter.

☐ Make sure the first sentence is indented.

☐ Make sure your sentences are complete.

☐ Other __**Can add other questions.**__

Publishing

Use this checklist to complete your paragraph.

Presentation

☐ Read your paragraph one more time. Make sure all the parts are there.

☐ Copy your paragraph onto a clean sheet of paper. Use your neatest handwriting.

☐ Share your paragraph with your classmates.

UNIT 4 Fossils • **Lesson 6** *Let's Go Dinosaur Tracking!*

Writing a Descriptive Paragraph

Objective: Students write a descriptive paragraph.

Prewriting

Who is the *audience* for your paragraph?

☐ your teacher

☐ a family member

☐ a friend

☐ other **Audience should be specific.**

What is the *purpose* of your paragraph?

☐ to describe what a dinosaur looked like

☐ to describe what fossils look like

☐ other **Topic should be specific.**

► **Writing a Descriptive Paragraph**

Objective: Students plan and draft a paragraph.

D E S C R I P T I V E   W R I T I N G

Plan the body of your paragraph. Write down what you will include in each sentence. Have students write ideas. They do not need to be complete sentences.

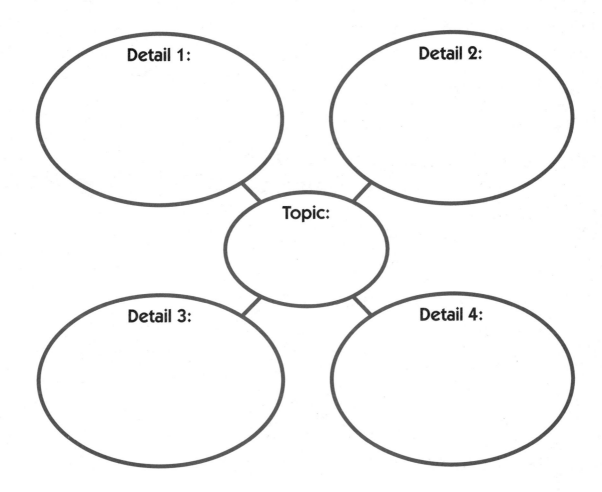

Detail 1:

Detail 2:

Topic:

Detail 3:

Detail 4:

Drafting

Write the first draft of your paragraph on lined notebook paper.

► **Writing a Descriptive Paragraph**

Revising

Read your paragraph. Use this checklist to make your paragraph better. Use proofreading marks to make changes.

Ideas

☐ Did you leave out anything you wanted to put in your paragraph?

☐ Do you have enough detail about the topic?

☐ Other **Can include additional questions.**

Organization

☐ Do you have a topic sentence?

☐ Are your sentences in order?

☐ Are all parts of your paragraph in place?

Word Choice

☐ Are there other words you can use to give more detail about the topic?

☐ Do the words you used give good descriptions?

Sentence Fluency

☐ Does each sentence add a new thought to your paragraph?

☐ Are there sentences you can delete?

Make all of your changes. Add anything else your paragraph needs.

Proofreading Marks

¶	Indent.
∧	Add something.
ℓ	Take out something.
≡	Make a capital letter.
/	Make a small letter.
sp◯	Check spelling.
⊙	Add a period.

▶ **Writing a Descriptive Paragraph**

DESCRIPTIVE WRITING

Objective: Students edit and proofread a paragraph.

Editing/Proofreading

Always proofread your paragraphs. Use this checklist to make sure you remember everything.

Conventions

☐ Check to make sure all your sentences are complete.

☐ Make sure each sentence begins with a capital letter.

☐ Make sure the first sentence is indented.

☐ Other __Can add questions about grammar, usage, and mechanics.__

Publishing

Use this checklist to complete your paragraph.

Presentation

☐ Copy your paragraph onto a clean sheet of paper. Use your neatest handwriting.

☐ Read your paragraph one more time. Make sure all the parts are there.

☐ Put your paragraph in a class collection.

UNIT 5 Courage • **Lesson I** *Molly the Brave and Me*

Writing a Personal Narrative

Objective: Students write a personal narrative.

Prewriting

Who is the *audience* for your personal narrative?

☐ your classmates

☐ your teacher

☐ your family

☐ a friend

☐ other **Audience should be specific.**

What is the *purpose* of your personal narrative?

☐ to tell about someone you admire

☐ to tell about a time you were brave

☐ other **Purpose for the writing needs to be clear and specific.**

UNIT 5 Courage • **Lesson 1** *Molly the Brave and Me*

Writing a Personal Narrative

Planning Your Narrative

When you write about events, you need to tell about them in the order they happened.

Students can fill in the following time line with events from their life.

Date:

———————|————————|————————|————————|———

Event:

Drafting

Write the first draft of your personal narrative on lined notebook paper. Follow your time line to write in a clear way.

UNIT 5 Courage • **Lesson 1** *Molly the Brave and Me*

Revising

Read your writing. Use the checklist below to improve your writing.

Ideas

☐ Do your ideas clearly show the cause and effect of events that you are describing?

Organization

☐ Does your writing have a clear topic sentence?

Word Choice

☐ Did you correctly use time and order words?

Sentence Fluency

☐ Will your reader be able to understand your narrative?

Voice

☐ Does your interest or excitement show in the way you tell about the events?

Other

☐ **Students should add other questions.**

Proofreading Marks

Mark	Meaning
⁋	Indent.
∧	Add something.
ℓ	Take out something.
≡	Make a capital letter.
/	Make a small letter.
⟲ᵖ	Check spelling.
⊙	Add a period.

Objective: Students revise their narratives.

UNIT 5 Courage • **Lesson I** *Molly the Brave and Me*

▶ Writing a Personal Narrative

Editing/Proofreading

Proofread your personal narrative. Use this checklist to help you fix any mistakes.

Conventions

☐ Is each paragraph indented?

☐ Does every sentence begin with a capital letter?

☐ Are all words and names of people and places correctly spelled?

☐ Does every sentence end with the correct punctuation?

☐ Other __Students should include other__ questions.

Publishing

Use this checklist to get your narrative ready to share.

Presentation

☐ Write or type a neat copy of your narrative.

☐ Include drawings, photographs, or a time line to help tell about your writing.

☐ Other **Add ideas for presentation.** _____

NARRATIVE WRITING

Objective: Students write a realistic story.

Writing a Realistic Story

Prewriting

Who is the *audience* for your story?

☐ your classmates

☐ your teacher

☐ your family

☐ a friend

☐ other **Audience should be specific.** _____

What is the *purpose* of your story?

☐ to write about a person who overcame his or her fear

☐ to write a made-up story that could really have happened

☐ other **Purpose for the writing needs to be clear and specific.**

Writing a Realistic Story

NARRATIVE WRITING

Objective: Students plan and draft their stories.

Planning Your Story

Decide who your characters will be. Where and when will the story take place? Plan your story by filling in the details on the story map below. Students should fill in their story maps.

characters:

setting:

PLOT

beginning: middle: end:

Drafting

Write the first draft of your realistic story on lined notebook paper. Put it in your Writing Folder.

Objective: Students revise their stories.

> **Writing a Realistic Story**

Revising

Read your story. Use the checklist below to make your writing better. Use editing marks to make any changes.

Ideas

☐ Are your characters realistic?

☐ Could your setting be a real place?

☐ Could the events in your story really happen?

Organization

☐ Does your story have a beginning, middle, and end?

Word Choice

☐ Did you correctly use time, order, and place words?

Sentence Fluency

☐ Will your reader be able to follow the events of your story?

Voice

☐ Does your story pull the readers in to make them feel a part of the story?

Other

☐ **Students should add other questions.**

Proofreading Marks	
¶	Indent.
∧	Add something.
ℓ	Take out something.
≡	Make a capital letter.
/	Make a small letter.
sp	Check spelling.
⊙	Add a period.

▶ **Writing a Realistic Story**

Editing/Proofreading

Proofread your story. Use this checklist to make sure you catch all of your mistakes.

Conventions

☐ Do sentences and proper nouns begin with capital letters?

☐ Is every word correctly spelled?

☐ Does every sentence end with the correct punctuation?

☐ Other **Students should include other** questions.

Publishing

Use this checklist to get your story ready to share.

Presentation

☐ Write or type a neat copy of your story.

☐ Include a drawing of a character or event from your story.

☐ Other **Add ideas for presentation.**

NARRATIVE WRITING

UNIT 5 Courage • **Lesson 3** *A Hole in the Dike*

Objective: Students write a fairy tale.

Writing a Fairy Tale

Prewriting

Who is the *audience* for your fairy tale?

☐ your classmates

☐ your teacher

☐ your family

☐ a friend

☐ other **Audience should be specific.**

What is the *purpose* of your fairy tale?

☐ to tell a story about a person who does something special

☐ to tell a story about make-believe characters and events

☐ other **Purpose for the writing needs to be clear and specific.**

UNIT 5 Courage • **Lesson 3** *A Hole in the Dike*

▶ **Writing a Fairy Tale**

NARRATIVE WRITING

Objective: Students plan and draft their fairy tales.

Planning Your Fairy Tale

Decide on the characters and setting of the story. Then plan the events of your fairy tale by filling in a story map.

Students should fill in their story maps.

characters:

setting:

PLOT

beginning:

middle:

end:

Drafting

Write the first draft of your fairy tale on lined notebook paper.

Objective: Students revise their fairy tales.

▶ **Writing a Fairy Tale**

Revising

Read your fairy tale. Use the checklist below to revise your writing.

Ideas

☐ Does your story have parts that make it a fairy tale?

☐ Are the settings, characters, and events imaginary?

Organization

☐ Is your fairy tale about a problem?

☐ Is the problem solved?

Word Choice

☐ Did you use words that paint a picture of your characters and what happens?

Sentence Fluency

☐ Will your reader be able to understand what is happening easily?

Voice

☐ Do you tell your fairy tale in an exciting and interesting way?

Other

☐ **Students should add other questions.**

Proofreading Marks

¶	Indent.
∧	Add something.
ℓ	Take out something.
≡	Make a capital letter.
/	Make a small letter.
⟲sp	Check spelling.
⊙	Add a period.

▶ **Writing a Fairy Tale**

NARRATIVE WRITING

Objective: Students edit and proofread their fairy tales.

Editing/Proofreading

Proofread your fairy tale. Use this checklist to help you find any mistakes in your writing.

Conventions

☐ Did you capitalize characters' names, place names, and the beginnings of sentences?

☐ Is every word correctly spelled?

☐ Does every sentence end with the correct punctuation?

☐ Other __Students should include other questions.__

Publishing

Use this checklist to get your fairy tale ready to share.

Presentation

☐ Write or type a neat copy of your fairy tale.

☐ Include a drawing of an important character or event from your fairy tale.

☐ Other __Add other ideas for presentation.__

UNIT 5 Courage • **Lesson 4** *Martin Luther King, Jr.*

Making a Picture Book

Objective: Students write and create a picture book.

Prewriting

Who is the *audience* for your picture book?

☐ a younger friend, brother, or sister

☐ your classmates

☐ your teacher

☐ other **Audience should be specific.**

What is the *purpose* of your picture book?

☐ to tell about someone you think is courageous

☐ to tell a story using words and pictures

☐ other **Purpose for the writing needs to be clear and specific.**

> **Making a Picture Book**

NARRATIVE WRITING

Objective: Students plan and draft their picture books.

Planning Your Picture Book

Choose your topic. Then draw a picture on your topic.

Topic: _____

Picture 1

Drafting

**Write the first draft of your picture book.
Use the picture you drew.**

Name _____ Date _____

Making a Picture Book

Objective: Students revise their picture books.

Revising

Read your picture book. Use the checklist below to make your writing better. Use editing marks to make any changes.

Ideas

☐ Do your words describe the pictures you want to show?

Organization

☐ Did you write something about each picture?

Word Choice

☐ Did you use simple words that young children can understand?

Sentence Fluency

☐ Do your events and information flow smoothly from one to another?

Voice

☐ Is your picture book interesting?

Other

☐ **Students should add other questions.**

Proofreading Marks

¶	Indent.
∧	Add something.
ℓ	Take out something.
≡	Make a capital letter.
/	Make a small letter.
sp	Check spelling.
⊙	Add a period.

▶ **Making a Picture Book**

NARRATIVE WRITING

Objective: Students edit and proofread their picture books.

Editing/Proofreading

Proofread your picture book. Use this checklist to help you correct mistakes in your writing.

Conventions

☐ Does every sentence begin with a capital letter?

☐ Did you capitalize people's names and place names?

☐ Are all words and special names or terms correctly spelled?

☐ Does every sentence end with the correct punctuation?

☐ Other **Students should include other questions.**

Publishing

Use this checklist to get your picture book ready to share.

Presentation

☐ Write or type a neat copy of your picture book.

☐ Place each drawing or photograph in the right position.

☐ Make a cover for your picture book and add a title.

☐ Other **Add ideas for presentation.**

UNIT 5 Courage • **Lesson 5** *The Empty Pot*

Writing a Realistic Story

Objective: Students write a realistic story.

Prewriting

Who is the *audience* for your story?

☐ your classmates

☐ your teacher

☐ your family

☐ a friend

☐ other **Audience should be specific.**

What is the *purpose* of your story?

☐ to write a story about someone who told the truth when no one else would

☐ to entertain your audience by telling a made-up story that seems real

☐ other **Purpose for the writing needs to be clear and specific.**

▶ **Writing a Realistic Story**

Planning Your Realistic Story

Decide on your characters. Where and **Students**
when will the story take place? Then fill in **should fill**
the details on your story map. **in their story maps.**

characters:

setting:

PLOT

beginning:
middle:
end:

Drafting

Write the first draft of your realistic story
on lined notebook paper.

NARRATIVE WRITING

UNIT 5 Courage • **Lesson 5** *The Empty Pot*

▶ Writing a Realistic Story

Objective: Students revise their stories.

Revising

Read your story. Use the checklist below to make your writing better.

Ideas

☐ Are your characters and setting realistic?

☐ Could the events in your story really happen?

Organization

☐ Are the events told in the right order?

Word Choice

☐ Did you use exact words that paint a picture?

Sentence Fluency

☐ Will your reader be able to follow your story?

Voice

☐ Is your story told with excitement?

Other

☐ **Students should add other questions.**

Proofreading Marks	
¶	Indent.
∧	Add something.
ℯ	Take out something.
≡	Make a capital letter.
/	Make a small letter.
ꜱⱷ	Check spelling.
⊙	Add a period.

► **Writing a Realistic Story**

Objective: Students edit and proofread their stories.

Editing/Proofreading

Proofread your story. Use this checklist to help you correct your mistakes.

Conventions

☐ Does every sentence and proper noun begin with a capital letter?

☐ Is every word correctly spelled?

☐ Does every sentence end with the correct punctuation?

☐ Other __Students should include other questions.__

Publishing

Use this checklist to get your story ready to share.

Presentation

☐ Write or type a neat copy of your story.

☐ Include a drawing that shows a character or event from your story.

☐ Other __Add ideas for presentation.__

NARRATIVE WRITING

Writing a Personal Narrative

Objective: Students write a personal narrative.

Prewriting

Who is the *audience* for your personal narrative?

☐ your classmates

☐ your teacher

☐ your family

☐ a friend

☐ other **Audience should be specific.**

What is the *purpose* for your personal narrative?

☐ to tell about a time you were brave

☐ to tell about something that has happened in your life

☐ other **Purpose for the writing needs to be clear and specific.**

NARRATIVE WRITING

Writing a Personal Narrative

Objective: Students plan and draft their narratives.

Planning Your Narrative

When you write about events in your life, you need to tell about them in the correct order. Fill in the web to organize your writing. **Students should fill in their webs.**

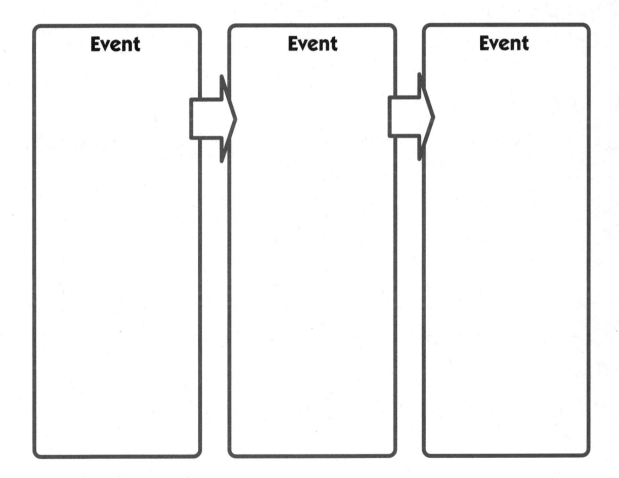

Event → Event → Event

Drafting

Write the first draft of your personal narrative on lined notebook paper.

UNIT 5   Courage • **Lesson 6** *Brave as a Mountain Lion*

Objective: Students revise their narratives.

▶ **Writing a Personal Narrative**

Revising

Read your writing. Use the checklist below to make your writing better.

Ideas

☐ Are there any ideas or details that you left out or that you need to add?

Organization

☐ Does your writing have an interesting topic sentence?

Word Choice

☐ Did you use details that tell what, where, when, and why?

Sentence Fluency

☐ Will your reader be able to understand your narrative?

Voice

☐ Are the events told in an interesting way?

Other

☐ **Students should add other questions.** _____

Proofreading Marks

¶	Indent.
∧	Add something.
ℓ	Take out something.
≡	Make a capital letter.
/	Make a small letter.
⊘	Check spelling.
⊙	Add a period.

UNIT 5 Courage • **Lesson 6** *Brave as a Mountain Lion*

▶ **Writing a Personal Narrative**

Editing/Proofreading

Proofread your personal narrative. Use this checklist to help you fix any mistakes.

Conventions

☐ Is each paragraph indented?

☐ Are all proper nouns and the beginning of each sentence capitalized?

☐ Are all words and names of people and places correctly spelled?

☐ Does every sentence end with the correct punctuation?

☐ Other **Students should include other questions.**

Publishing

Use this checklist to get your narrative ready to share.

Presentation

☐ Write or type a neat copy of your narrative.

☐ Include drawings, photographs, or a time line to help tell about your writing.

☐ Other **Add ideas for presentation.**

Objective: Students write persuasive letters.

Writing a Persuasive Letter

Prewriting

Who is the *audience* for your letter?

☐ a friend

☐ a teacher

☐ your family

☐ other **Audience should be specific.**

What is the *purpose* of your writing?

☐ to get someone to read a story

☐ to persuade someone to think, act, or feel a certain way

☐ other **Purpose should be clearly stated.**

Name _____ Date _____

► Writing a Persuasive Letter

Planning Your Letter

Plan the body of your letter. Write down reasons that support your topic.

Objective: Students plan and draft their letters.

Reason #1
Reason #2
Reason #3

Drafting

Write the first draft of your letter on lined notebook paper. Put it in your Writing Folder.

PERSUASIVE WRITING

► **Writing a Persuasive Letter**

Objective: Students revise their letters.

Revising

Read your letter. Use this checklist to make your letter better. Use proofreading marks to make changes.

Ideas

☐ Does your topic persuade others to do something?

☐ Do you have good reasons to support your topic?

Organization

☐ Did you include a greeting, closing, and date in your letter?

☐ Did you write your topic in the first sentence?

Word Choice

☐ Are there other words you can use to give more detail?

Sentence Fluency

☐ Are all your sentences complete?

☐ Are your sentences easy to read?

Voice

☐ Think about your reader. Does your letter sound polite?

☐ Other **Can include additional questions.** _____

Make all of your changes. Add anything else your letter needs.

Proofreading Marks	
¶	Indent.
∧	Add something.
ℓ	Take out something.
≡	Make a capital letter.
/	Make a small letter.
sᴘ	Check spelling.
⊙	Add a period.

▶ **Writing a Persuasive Letter**

Objective: Students edit and proofread their letters.

Editing/Proofreading

Always proofread your letters. Use this checklist to make sure you remember everything.

Conventions

☐ Check for spelling errors.

☐ Make sure proper names and beginnings of sentences start with a capital letter.

☐ Other **Can add other concerns.** _____

Publishing

Use this checklist to get your letter ready to mail.

Presentation

☐ Make a neatly typed or written final copy.

☐ Read your letter one more time. Make sure all the parts of the letter are there.

☐ Sign your letter.

☐ Add a stamp to your letter and mail it.

PERSUASIVE WRITING

Objective: Students write persuasive paragraphs.

UNIT 6 **Our Country and Its People • Lesson 2** *New Hope*

Writing a Persuasive Paragraph

Prewriting

Who is the *audience* for your paragraph?

☐ a friend

☐ a teacher

☐ your family

☐ other __Audience should be specific.__

What is the *purpose* of your writing?

☐ to persuade someone to come to the United States

☐ to get someone to do something

☐ other __Purpose should be clearly stated.__

Objective: Students plan and draft their paragraphs.

> **Writing a Persuasive Paragraph**

Planning Your Paragraph

Plan the body of your paragraph. Write down what you will include in each sentence. Have students write ideas. They do not need to be complete sentences.

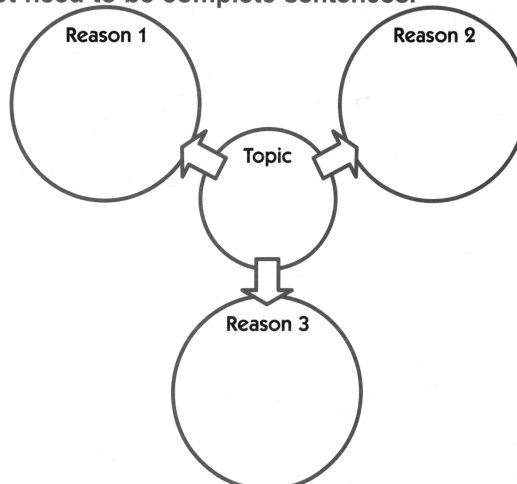

Reason 1

Reason 2

Topic

Reason 3

Drafting

Write the first draft of your paragraph on lined notebook paper. Put it in your Writing Folder.

PERSUASIVE WRITING

Objective: Students revise their paragraphs.

Revising

▶ **Writing a Persuasive Paragraph**

Read your paragraph. Use this checklist to make your writing better. Use proofreading marks to make changes.

Ideas

☐ Does your topic persuade others to do something?

☐ Do you have good reasons to support your topic?

Organization

☐ Did you write your topic in the first sentence?

Word Choice

☐ Are there other words you can use to give more detail?

Sentence Fluency

☐ Are all your sentences complete?

☐ Are your sentences easy to read?

Voice

☐ Think about your reader. Do your paragraphs sound polite?

☐ Other __**Can include additional questions.**__

Make all of your changes. Add anything else your paragraph needs.

Proofreading Marks	
⊬	Indent.
∧	Add something.
ℓ	Take out something.
≡	Make a capital letter.
/	Make a small letter.
✺	Check spelling.
⊙	Add a period.

► **Writing a Persuasive Paragraph**

PERSUASIVE WRITING

Objective: Students edit and proofread their paragraphs.

Editing/Proofreading

Always proofread your writing. Use this checklist to make sure you remember everything.

Conventions

☐ Check for spelling errors.

☐ Make sure beginnings of sentences start with a capital letter.

☐ Other **Can add concerns about grammar, usage, and mechanics specific to a persuasive paragraph.**

Publishing

Use this checklist to finish your paragraph.

Presentation

☐ Make a neatly typed or written final copy.

☐ Read your paragraph one more time. Make sure all the parts are there.

Objective: Students write persuasive commercials.

Writing a Persuasive Commercial

Prewriting

Who is the *audience* for your commercial?

☐ your school

☐ your classmates

☐ other __Audience should be specific.__

What is the *purpose* of your commercial?

☐ to get someone to vote

☐ to persuade someone to do something

☐ other __Purpose should be clearly stated.__

Name _____ Date _____

▶ **Writing a Persuasive Commercial**

Planning Your Commercial

Have students write ideas. They do not need to be complete sentences.

Plan your commercial. Write down what you will include in each sentence.

Write words for the first person in your commercial. ▶

Write words for the second person in your commercial. ▶

Write words for the third person in your commercial. ▶

Write words for the fourth person in your commercial. ▶

Drafting

Write the first draft of your commercial script on lined notebook paper. Put it in your Writing Folder.

Objective: Students plan and draft their scripts for their commercials.

PERSUASIVE WRITING

Name _____ Date _____

▶ Writing a Persuasive Commercial

Revising

Read your commercial script. Use this checklist to make it better. Use proofreading marks to make changes.

Ideas

☐ Does your topic persuade others to do something?

☐ Do you have good reasons to support your topic?

Organization

☐ Do you tell your topic right away?

☐ Is your topic clear?

☐ Does everyone in your group help in some way?

Word Choice

☐ Are there other words you can use to give more detail?

Sentence Fluency

☐ Are all your sentences complete?

Voice

☐ Think about your audience. Is your commercial polite?

☐ Other ___**Can include other ideas.**___

Make all of your changes. Add props if you would like.

Proofreading Marks	
¶	Indent.
∧	Add something.
ℓ	Take out something.
≡	Make a capital letter.
/	Make a small letter.
⊘	Check spelling.
⊙	Add a period.

Objective: Students revise their scripts.

▶ Writing a Persuasive Commercial

(sidebar) Objective: Students edit and proofread their scripts.

(sidebar) **PERSUASIVE WRITING**

Editing/Proofreading

Always proofread your scripts. Careless mistakes make a bad impression. Use this checklist to make sure you remember everything.

Conventions

☐ Check for spelling errors.

☐ Make sure proper names and beginnings of sentences start with a capital letter.

☐ Other **Can add other concerns.** _____

Presentation

☐ Add props if you can.

☐ Perform your commercial.

Objective: Students write persuasive letters.

Writing a Persuasive Letter

Prewriting

Who is the *audience* for your letter?

☐ a friend

☐ a teacher

☐ your family

☐ other <u>**Audience should be specific.**</u>

What is the *purpose* of your letter?

☐ to persuade your teacher to take the class to see the Statue of Liberty

☐ to persuade someone to do something

☐ other <u>**Purpose should be clearly stated.**</u>

Objective: Students plan and draft their letters.

PERSUASIVE WRITING

▶ **Writing a Persuasive Letter**

Planning Your Letter

Plan the body of your letter. Write down what you will include in each sentence.

1. Write your topic.	▶ **Topic should be specific.**
2. Write detail to support topic.	▶
3. Write detail to support topic.	▶
4. Write detail to support topic.	▶

Drafting

Write the first draft of your letter on lined notebook paper.

Objective: Students revise their letters.

▶ **Writing a Persuasive Letter**

Revising

Read your letter. Use this checklist to make your letter better. Use proofreading marks to make changes.

Ideas

☐ Does your topic persuade others to do something?

☐ Do you have good reasons to support your topic?

Organization

☐ Does your letter have a greeting, a closing, and a date?

☐ Did you write your topic in the first sentence?

Word Choice

☐ Are there other words you can use to give more detail?

Sentence Fluency

☐ Are all your sentences complete?

☐ Are your sentences easy to read?

Voice

☐ Think about your audience. Does your letter persuade your reader?

☐ Other **Can include other ideas.** _____

Make all of your changes. Add anything else your letter needs.

Proofreading Marks	
¶	Indent.
∧	Add something.
ℓ	Take out something.
=	Make a capital letter.
/	Make a small letter.
sp	Check spelling.
⊙	Add a period.

UNIT 6 Our Country and Its People • **Lesson 4** *The Story of the Statue of Liberty*

▶ **Writing a Persuasive Letter**

Objective: Students edit and proofread their letters.

PERSUASIVE WRITING

Editing/Proofreading

Always proofread your letters. Use this checklist to make sure you remember everything.

Conventions

☐ Check for spelling errors.

☐ Make sure proper names and beginnings of sentences start with capital letters.

☐ Other **Can add other concerns.** _____

Publishing

Use this checklist to get your letter ready to mail.

Presentation

☐ Make a neatly typed or written final copy.

☐ Sign your letter.

☐ Read your letter one more time. Make sure all the parts of the letter are there.

☐ Give your letter to your teacher or someone to read.

Making a Persuasive Poster

Objective: Students create posters.

Prewriting

Who is the *audience* for your poster?

☐ your school

☐ your classmates

☐ other __Audience should be specific.__

What is the *purpose* of your poster?

☐ to express pride in your heritage

☐ to get someone to feel a certain way

☐ other __Purpose should be clearly stated.__

▶ **Making a Persuasive Poster**

Planning Your Poster

Plan your poster. Write down what you will include. Have students write ideas. They do not need to be complete sentences.

Write what you want to say.

Draw pictures to go along with your topic.

Objective: Students plan their posters.

Drafting

Write the first draft of your poster on a sheet of lined notebook paper.

PERSUASIVE WRITING

► **Making a Persuasive Poster**

Objective: Students revise their posters.

Revising

Read your poster. Use this checklist to make it better. Use proofreading marks to make changes.

Ideas

☐ Does your topic persuade others to do something?

☐ Do you have good reasons to support your topic?

☐ Do your pictures match your topic?

Organization

☐ Did you write your topic at the top of the poster?

Word Choice

☐ Are there other words you can use to give more detail?

Voice

☐ Do you sound proud of your heritage or topic?

☐ Will your readers be persuaded?

Other

☐ **Can include other ideas.** _____

Make all of your changes. Add anything else your poster needs.

Proofreading Marks

⌶	Indent.
∧	Add something.
ℯ	Take out something.
≡	Make a capital letter.
/	Make a small letter.
sp	Check spelling.
⊙	Add a period.

▶ Making a Persuasive Poster

Editing/Proofreading

Objective: Students edit and proofread their posters.

Always proofread your posters. Use this checklist to make sure you remember everything.

Conventions

☐ Check for spelling errors.

☐ Make sure beginnings of sentences start with a capital letter.

☐ Other **Can add other concerns.** _____

Publishing

Use this checklist to finish your poster.

Presentation

☐ Make a neatly written final copy.

☐ Did you use colored pencils or markers to make your pictures more interesting?

☐ Look at your poster one more time. Make sure all the parts are there.

☐ Present your poster to your class.

PERSUASIVE WRITING

Objective: Students write persuasive paragraphs.

Writing a Persuasive Paragraph

Prewriting

Who is the *audience* for your paragraph?

☐ a friend

☐ a teacher

☐ your family

☐ other __**Audience should be specific.**__

What is the *purpose* of your paragraph?

☐ to persuade others that your hometown is a nice place to live

☐ to get someone to feel a certain way

☐ to get someone to act a certain way

☐ other __**Purpose should be clearly stated.**__

▶ Writing a Persuasive Paragraph

PERSUASIVE WRITING

Objective: Students plan and draft their paragraphs.

Planning Your Paragraph

Plan the body of your paragraph. Write Have students down what you will include in each write ideas. They sentence. do not need to be complete sentences.

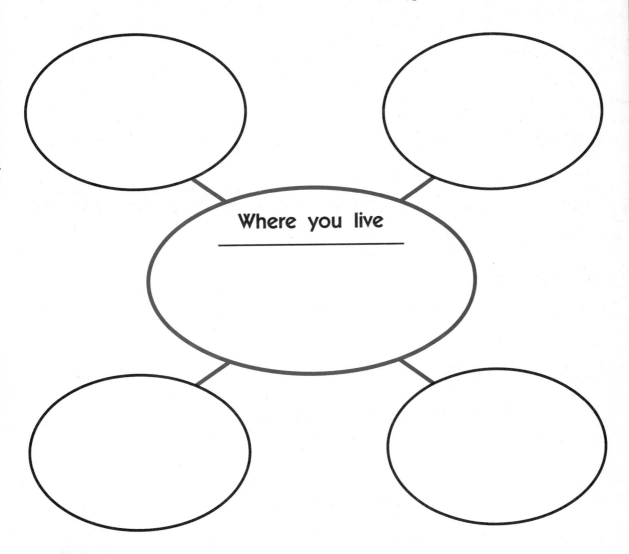

Where you live

Drafting

Write the first draft of your paragraph on lined notebook paper.

Objective: Students revise their paragraphs.

▶ **Writing a Persuasive Paragraph**

Revising

Read your paragraph. Use this checklist to make your writing better. Use proofreading marks to make changes.

Ideas

☐ Does your topic persuade others to do something?

☐ Do you have good reasons to support your topic?

Organization

☐ Did you write your topic in the first sentence?

Word Choice

☐ Are there other words you can use to give more detail?

Sentence Fluency

☐ Are all your sentences complete?

☐ Are your sentences easy to read?

Voice

☐ Did you sound proud of your hometown?

☐ Will your readers be proud of your hometown?

☐ Other __Can include other ideas.__

Make all of your changes. Add anything else your paragraph needs.

Proofreading Marks

¶	Indent.
∧	Add something.
ℓ	Take out something.
≡	Make a capital letter.
/	Make a small letter.
sp⟳	Check spelling.
⊙	Add a period.

UNIT 6 Our Country and Its People • **Lesson 6** *A Piece of Home*

Writing a Persuasive Paragraph

PERSUASIVE WRITING

Editing/Proofreading

Always proofread your writing. Use this checklist to make sure you remember everything.

Conventions

☐ Check for spelling errors.

☐ Make sure beginnings of sentences start with a capital letter.

☐ Other **Can add other concerns.** _____

Publishing

Use this checklist to finish your paragraph.

Presentation

☐ Make a neatly typed or written final copy.

☐ Read your paragraph one more time. Make sure all the parts are there.

☐ Share your paragraph with your friends or classmates.

Objective: Students create persuasive posters.

Making a Persuasive Poster

Prewriting

Who is the *audience* for your poster?

☐ your school

☐ your classmates

☐ other ___Audience should be specific.___

What is the *purpose* of your poster?

☐ to get someone to buy bagels

☐ to get someone to buy something

☐ to get someone to act a certain way

☐ other ___Purpose should be clearly stated.___

UNIT 6 Our Country and Its People • **Lesson 7** *Jalapeño Bagels*

Objective: Students plan and draft their posters.

P E R S U A S I V E   W R I T I N G

Making a Persuasive Poster

Planning Your Poster

Plan your poster. Write down what you will include. **Have students write ideas. They do not need to be complete sentences.**

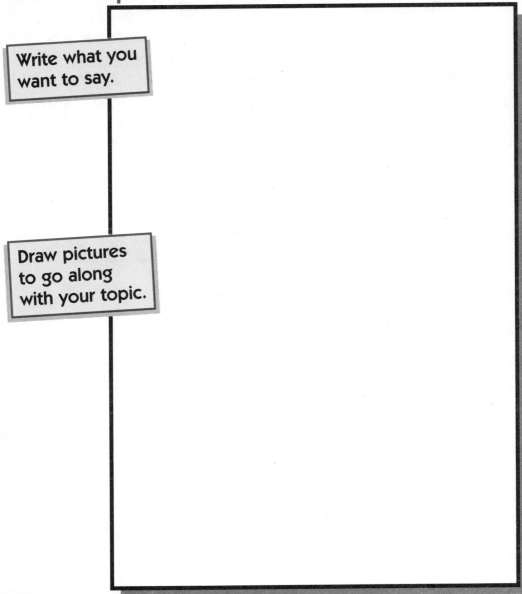

Write what you want to say.

Draw pictures to go along with your topic.

Drafting

Write the first draft of your poster on lined notebook paper.

Objective: Students revise their posters.

Revising

▶ **Making a Persuasive Poster**

Read your poster. Use this checklist to make it better. Use proofreading marks to make changes.

Ideas

☐ Does your topic persuade others to do something?

☐ Do you have good reasons to support your topic?

☐ Do your pictures match your topic?

Organization

☐ Did you write your topic at the top of the poster?

Word Choice

☐ Are there other words you can use to give more detail?

Voice

☐ Think about your reader. Do your words sound polite?

☐ Will your readers want to buy what you are selling?

Other

☐ **Can include other ideas.** _____

Proofreading Marks	
¶	Indent.
∧	Add something.
℮	Take out something.
≡	Make a capital letter.
/	Make a small letter.
⬭ sp	Check spelling.
⊙	Add a period.

▶ **Making a Persuasive Poster**

Editing/Proofreading

Objective: Students edit and proofread their posters.

Always proofread your posters. Use this checklist to make sure you remember everything.

Conventions

☐ Check for spelling errors.

☐ Make sure beginnings of sentences start with a capital letter.

☐ Other **Can add other concerns.** _____

Publishing

Use this checklist to finish your poster.

Presentation

☐ Make a neatly written final copy.

☐ Look at your poster one more time. Make sure all the parts are there.

☐ Share your poster.

PERSUASIVE WRITING

Cumulative Checklists

Revising

Ideas

☐ Did you say everything you wanted to say?

☐ Are your ideas interesting and unique?

☐ Did you take out information that you don't need?

☐ Did you add important information?

☐ Will your readers want to continue reading what you wrote?

Organization

☐ Do you have an interesting topic sentence?

☐ Did you stay on the topic?

☐ Do you have supporting details?

☐ Is everything in the right order?

☐ Did you use your graphic organizer or prewriting plans?

☐ Do you have a good beginning and ending?

Voice

☐ Does your writing sound like you wrote it?

☐ Is your writing polite?

☐ Did you say how you really feel?

☐ Will your readers feel like they know you?

Revising

Word Choice

☐ Did you use the best words to say what you mean?

☐ Can you use time and order words to make your writing better?

☐ Did you define hard words for your readers?

☐ Can you use place or location words to make your writing better?

☐ Did you use a thesaurus to find better words?

☐ Did you look up words you don't know in a dictionary?

Sentence Fluency

☐ Can you combine your sentences so they are easier to read?

☐ Did you use transition words?

☐ Do you have complete sentences?

☐ Can you elaborate to give your readers more details or information?

☐ Did you use different types of sentences?

☐ Can you use dialogue instead of just telling what someone said?

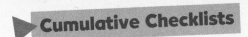

Editing/Proofreading

Unit 1 Grammar and Usage

Lesson 1 ☐ Nouns: Common and Proper

Lesson 2 ☐ Pronouns: Subject and Object

Lesson 3 ☐ Action Verbs

Lesson 4 ☐ Possessive Nouns and Pronouns

Unit 2 Mechanics

Lesson 1 ☐ Capitalization: Beginnings of Sentences

Lesson 2 ☐ Commas in Greeting and Closing

Lesson 3 ☐ Capitalization: Months, Days

Lesson 4 ☐ Punctuation: Commas in a Series

Lesson 5 ☐ Punctuation: Quotation Marks and Underlining

Unit 3 Grammar and Usage

Lesson 1 ☐ Sentences and End Marks

Lesson 2 ☐ Linking and Helping Verbs

Lesson 3 ☐ Subject/Verb Agreement

Lesson 4 ☐ Parts of Sentences

Lesson 5 ☐ Complete Sentences

Editing/Proofreading

Unit 4 Grammar and Usage

Lesson 1 ☐ Adjectives

Lesson 2 ☐ Contractions

Lesson 3 ☐ Verb Tenses

Lesson 4 ☐ Nouns: Singular and Plural

Lesson 5 ☐ Adverbs

Unit 5 Grammar, Usage, and Mechanics

Lesson 1 ☐ Capitalization: Proper Nouns

Lesson 2 ☐ Conjunctions and Interjections

Lesson 4 ☐ Capitalization: Titles and Initials

Lesson 3 ☐ Punctuation: Commas in Dialogue

Lesson 5 ☐ Punctuation: Apostrophes and Colons

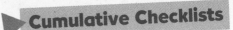

Publishing

Unit 2 Personal Writing

☐ Did you print or write on only one side of the paper?

☐ Did you make a neat, clean copy of your writing?

☐ Can you share your work with your class?

☐ Could you mail your writing to a friend or company?

☐ Did you put your work in a class collection for the school to see?

☐ Can you copy your writing on fancy paper?

☐ Did you use computer clip art for decorations?

Unit 3 Expository Writing

☐ Did you include drawings or maps to make your writing easier to follow?

☐ Did you share your writing with the class?

☐ Can you make a colorful cover for your work?

☐ Could you add photographs to show the topic of your writing?

☐ Did you use the computer to publish your writing?

PUBLISHING CHECKLIST

Publishing

Unit 4 Poetry and Descriptive Writing

☐ Can you make your poem into a shape?

☐ Did you sing or perform your writing?

☐ Could you make pictures or use computer clip art to make your writing more interesting?

☐ Did you add your writing to a class collection of writing?

Unit 5 Narrative Writing

☐ Did you include photographs with your writing?

☐ Did you share your work with your class?

☐ Could you perform your writing?

☐ Did you make a colorful cover for your work?

☐ Did you draw pictures of the characters in your writing?

Unit 6 Persuasive Writing

☐ Did you mail your work to someone you know?

☐ Can you perform your work with other people in a group?

☐ Did you use paint, crayons, or markers to make your work appealing to your readers?

☐ Did you use an atlas to find places you mention in your writing? Can you show others those places?

☐ Did you make a colorful cover for your writing?

☐ Can you print your writing on the computer at school?